Danni –
Hop
of the
book!

Love,
Lori

Hold It Like A Football...Just Remember Not to Spike It

To order additional copies, please contact us.
BookSurge, LLC
www.booksurge.com
1-866-308-6235
orders@booksurge.com

Hold It Like A Football...Just Remember Not to Spike It

And Other Pearls of Wisdom on Becoming a Father

Pete Slease

2006

Hold It Like A Football...Just
Remember Not to Spike It

Table of Contents

To Jenny: with you in my life everything is possible. Thank you.

To Emma Grace: your kicks, rolls, and turns made mommy just uncomfortable (and crazy) enough to give daddy some great material. I owe you.

Chapter 1

What Do Two Pink Lines Mean Again?

So, you just found out that your wife is pregnant. When I found out that my wife was pregnant the thoughts that ran through my head were, "Oh my god! My boys can swim!"; and, "Awesome, a baby!" Your reaction may have been, "Let's call everyone to tell them you're 9 days pregnant!" which was followed by.... "Damn, now I bet she'll *really* want me to re-paint that room" . Or, "Holy crap! If she has the baby before the end of the year, I'll get that great tax break!" Just remember, though, that only part of these reactions can be shared aloud, because if you start saying these things to your wife, oh you'll face the wrath. And believe me, you don't want to face the wrath this early. You'll see plenty of that in the months ahead ... why push her buttons now?

But, I digress, as most men are known to do. You see, this men's guide has a very rough format to it. It's designed for the guy that wants to flip around to whatever pertains to him. Your wife's acting more insane than usual? Proceed to the first page of the chapter on Mood Swings. What's that? Your wife just ate a cold piece of leftover meatloaf for breakfast? Flip to Cravings. You say your wife's more flatulent than you are after a wing-eating contest? Bodily Functions is the place to go, my friend.

Yes, that's right, I called you friend. Because in this crazy time called pregnancy, all men set aside their differences, political, sports teams, and otherwise, and join together in the misery and joy (and it's mostly joy) of your significant other's months of carrying around that alien inside of her.

The purpose of this book is to give you some solace in knowing that you're not the only one going through what you're going through. Since the dawn of man, pregnant women have had irrational emotional outbursts, and men have taken the brunt of the explosions.

I know you're excited! You have to be, I mean, you're about to become the proud papa of a little baby boy or girl. But, if you're like most guys, you speak before you think, and that tends to get you in trouble. You know, the audible, closed-lipped "Um-hum" as a hot girl walks by; or, after your wife puts on a few pounds and asks if she looks fat, you start by saying, "Well ...". Never a good thing. If you didn't think she was starting to push maximum density, you'd say, "No, honey, you look great!", not, "Well ...", which can only lead to sentences like, "Well, you don't look that bad." *SLAP* With that in mind, your reaction to the news of pregnancy should be total excitement, and it probably was, so you should be fine. If, from this point forward, you make sure to only think, and not verbalize, your thoughts, you'll be in great shape.

Now, where was I? Oh yeah! You just found out that you're going to be a father. Here are my Top 10 reactions of men and women:

<u>Women</u>

1) I'm going to be a mommy!

2) I wonder if it's a boy or a girl ... or twins!

3) I'm not going to be one of those fat pregnant women! I'm going to eat right & exercise every day!

4) Maternity clothes are sooo cute! I can't wait to go shopping!

5) I better get started picking out baby clothes, too!

6) I guess that explains why I had a hankering for cottage cheese and chocolate sauce!

7) Finally, a chance for *him* to wait on *me*!

8) No more job; I'm going to be a stay-at-home-mom!

9) He may not know it yet, but he's going to have to share in the diaper duties ... and 2 a.m. feedings ... and ...

10) Now I get to turn his rec room into the baby's playroom!

<u>Men</u>

1) I'm going to be a daddy!

2) Does this mean that we're never going to have sex again?

3) I hope she doesn't get too fat ...

4) Great, now she's got *another* excuse to go shopping!

5) Let's see, if the baby's born in 8 months, then he'll be eligible for the NFL draft in 20 years, 8 months ... which means I can retire in 20 years, 9 months! Sweet!

6) Nine months of built-in designated driver ...

7) Does that mean that the in-laws are going to start stopping by totally unannounced?

8) Is this going to completely cut out my ability to play PlayStation every Saturday morning for hours on end?

9) I better not have to share in any of the diaper duties ...

10) Where's this kid going to play? 'Cause we're not touching my rec room!

All of these reactions are pretty typical for men and women. Your wife's probably going to be more excited than you right now for the simple fact that most women prepare for motherhood from the time they can stand on two feet and hold something at the same time ... and that "something" usually is? What else, a doll. And the boys? Well, you can't get most little guys within thirty feet of a doll, so we were probably clutching a baseball or football, which helps to explain why you still play Wednesday night softball and help run your fantasy football league. Hey, you have to give women credit for the simple fact that one of their greatest goals in life (motherhood) is a little more attainable than ours (professional athlete).

Anyway, don't sweat it if you're not ecstatic yet. Chances are you're really excited about being a daddy, but it hasn't completely sunk in yet. And that's okay. It'll happen. Believe me, when your wife goes from Cinderella to Godzilla to Sleeping Beauty in under a minute flat, it'll hit you like a ton of bricks. You see, and it's best to get this in your head right now, your wife has something *growing* inside of her. And, no there's nothing to compare it to, not even the rumbling you get after you eat Mexican food. Your significant other has a living, breathing human being growing inside of her, and there's not one minute of one day that goes by without her knowing it. Even in the early stages when you can't see that she's pregnant, she's thinking about it constantly. Learn that now. The sooner you do, the better the months ahead will be.

Now if you were looking for one of those touchy-feely self-help books, put this book back down. This isn't your typical Dr. Phil book. I'm writing it just like you're seeing it and feeling it. This is a written documentary, if you will, and it's not watered down. I'm not going to beat around the bush; I'm going to tell it like it is. "Is my wife going to get fat" ....YES, some get huge! "Is my wife going to yell at me".......YES, even more than she usually does!

Parenthood is probably the greatest joy in the world, but before you get there you'll need to endure the pregnant months with your missus. This book will help guide you through the minefield of pregnancy, and hopefully help you avoid some of those missteps that can mean sofa-time for daddy.

Chapter 2

Sickness, Just Sickness

Well, if your significant other is like most women during pregnancy, chances are pretty good that she's going to hurl at some point during the first few months of pregnancy. In fact, she's probably going to do more than just puke, and it isn't necessarily in the morning. I can still remember getting the "Honey, I can't keep anything down" phone calls. They usually went something like,

"How're you feeling, sweetie?"

"Well, I ate an omelet this morning, but I threw it right back up, and now I've got really bad diarrhea."

"Wow. That officially qualifies as more information than I needed to know."

Seriously, it doesn't matter how demure your wife was when you met, dated, and got married, she is going to share everything with you now. So get used to it.

So this morning sickness thing, what's it all about?

Well, I'll be honest, I'm not a doctor and I don't claim to be, either, but this much I do know: your wife's hormones are raging. She's going through changes that we wouldn't be able to handle; and, she's got a little critter growing inside of her. It's pretty understandable why it's going to take a little while for her to adjust to the changes.

Before we move on, you have to understand that morning sickness is a misnomer. They should really call it sickness. Just plain ol' sickness, because it can hit at anytime, and does.

Now the term morning sickness means different things for different women, but for most women, at the very least, it means some nausea. Now, I'm sure there are women out there who can proudly say, "Oh, I never felt a thing during my whole pregnancy ... in fact, I was more active than normal!" But these are probably the same ladies who brag, "I only gained seven pounds during my entire pregnancy!", and "I didn't even need an epidural during the labor! I went completely natural!". And to you women, I say, "Congratulations. With comments like those, you move men like me, who endured several months of set-your-clock-by-the-timing vomit sessions, that much closer to jumping off the nearest bridge.

Chances are morning sickness will only affect *you* a little bit. Unless you're one of those "Can I hold your hair back while you boot" type of guys, you won't have to take much action during this period. Try to be reasonable, though. I mean, this isn't the time to subject your wife to Fear Factor marathons where the tamest competition is pig-bile guzzling. Same goes with those post meal burps and farts you may be used to at this point in the relationship. You'll be amazed what sends her over the edge now. It can be smells, sights, tastes, all kinds of things. Just expect the unexpected.

Case in point: my wife is a big fan of pistachios. Loves 'em. I can still remember, a few days before we found out that she was pregnant, we had a thirty minute conversation in the kitchen where she stood over the trash can shucking pistachios and popping them into her mouth like some giant member of the squirrel family. *Thirty* minutes, folks. Do you have any idea what it's like to witness something like that? Believe me, I was deeply disturbed about that, but when I found out she was pregnant, oh, it made all the sense in the world. She loves pistachios, and she was just showing me that.

Now, fast forward two weeks, when we were fixing dinner together, and I offered her some pistachios, and she just about lost it. No idea why, but for some reason, the thought alone made her almost throw up. I thought I was being nice. Hell I even offered to shell them for her, considering it would've saved me from having to witness her squirrel impersonation, but she ran to the bathroom, and nearly booted.

Funny thing is, at the three month mark, she was back to eating pistachios again. That whole, "don't bring those things near me or else I'll hurl in your lap" thing? Gone. She was back to normal. Shelling pistachios over the trash can like Bullwinkle's Rocky.

Thankfully, this phase of the pregnancy shouldn't last the duration. Speaking from personal experience, it only lasted (easy for me to say "only", right?) about three months. After that, almost every food that she was able to eat before the pregnancy stayed down pretty well. In fact, there were some new foods added to the mix, which leads me to ...

Chapter 3

Midnight Run

A little background: the missus is healthy, and eats normally. No, I'm not trying to be kind, and describe her as "healthy" when I'm really trying to say that she's a chunk. I mean that she's healthy. She's got a great figure, and she eats what she wants, but almost always in normal portions, never more than she needs to.

Me on the other hand, I eat what's in front of me regardless of how full I am. You know what I'm talking about. You're at a restaurant, and even though you know you've got a T-bone with mashed potatoes coming out in ten minutes, you can't resist eating seven more wings, or polishing off the last third of the nachos. Then, there's no way you can waste that steak and potatoes, so you make one simple adjustment (read: loosen the belt), and you're all set. Yeah, my wife doesn't eat like that.

The other thing is she pretty much just eats when most other people eat: breakfast, lunch and dinner. Sometimes, not often, but sometimes she'd be a little kooky and have cheese and crackers after work *egad*, but she wasn't an overeater, and she didn't eat all the time.

Well, once again, welcome to Bizarro World, where up is down, left is right, black is white, and your wife is crazy.

Don't worry, mine is too. Want some examples? Okay, the night before my wife took the first of four pregnancy tests do you want to know what she had for dinner? Two cans of large, pitted black olives. Nothing else. Just the olives. Straight out of the can. She left the evidence right there on the coffee table: two empty cans of large, pitted black olives and a fork. I already told you about the pistachio-shucking record that she set, so there's another. How about the pickles? Always a lover of pickles, my wife started eating six and seven in a sitting. And we're not talking the little hamburger dill slices, either, I mean the big honkin' fat, whole pickles.

And sweets, too. My wife's never been a big sweets eater, but when she does eat sweets, it's usually a bite or two of low fat ice cream or frozen yogurt. Fast forward to month three of the pregnancy and we now have mass chocolate consumption. We're talking Snickers bars, chocolate-chip cookies, just about anything chocolate. I knew she'd officially gone to the Land of No Return when she ordered a dessert called the Great Wall of Chocolate. Any time you order something that's named after one of the 7 Wonders of the World, you know it's going to be enormous. And when you finish every last bite, well, you just may have yourself an addiction on your hands.

As for the timing of the cravings, there's no rhyme or reason for when she'll be hungry. Just bank on your wife being a pretty good impersonation of you from the ages of 12-25: a never-satisfied eating machine. "Good night" and "good morning" will be replaced with "I'm hungry". In fact, "I'm hungry" will become a sort of mantra, if you will.

In the morning you'll ask, "How'd you sleep?"

She'll respond, "Pretty well. But I'm hungry."

You'll call her from work (the time doesn't matter), "How is your day going?"

She'll say, "Not too bad. I'm hungry, though."

You'll come home from work and say, "It's been a long day, honey. I'm really hungry."

And she'll respond, "Good, because I'm hungry, too."

I truly think this aspect of the pregnancy is preparing you for fatherhood, because you'll have to be like an "always prepared" boy scout and have a little bag of cereal or animal crackers at the ready. In fact, it's not a bad idea to have this kind of thing ready for your significant other during the pregnancy. It'll be good practice for you, and you'll keep her from gnawing on table legs while you wait to be served in a restaurant.

The types of foods that your wife will crave are anyone's guess. Some women crave exactly what they normally eat, just in massive quantities and at strange times. Others take on completely new cravings. Just remember, though, massive quantities, and not on any schedule that you're used to. And the cravings will change more often than you change your socks. In the course of a week, my wife went from macaroni and cheese to handfuls of pickles to frozen yogurt with loads of toppings to Cheerios and back to mac and cheese. To cope with this, and to prevent frequent market visits, it's best to recreate, as closely as possible, every single aisle of the grocery store. And be prepared to stock up on something, only to have your significant other tell you in no uncertain terms that, "The thought of that makes me want to throw up". Guess you're stuck eating those gingersnap cookies, buster.

I'll tell you, as cravings go, Boy Scout training helps quite a bit. And if you're not the "Be Prepared" type? Well, be prepared to make midnight runs to 7-11 for cheese-in-a-can and Oreos.

Update*: Month 6- Boy, the wheels have come off now. I think my wife is trying that Hollywood diet where you eat eleven small meals a day. You know the one. The diet that's totally unreasonable because you'd basically be eating all day long, but none of the meals would consist of anything more than a slice of cantaloupe, or half of a sesame seed bagel? Yeah, well, that's what my wife's started doing ... except these aren't small meals. Case in point: yesterday she gave me the rundown on the eating for the day, and this is no exaggeration:

* since I'm writing this as it happens, it's only fair to give you as many updates as possible on many of the subjects in this book, hence, the Updates.

Breakfast (8:00 a.m.)
sausage, egg and cheese on a croissant
toasted bagel with cream cheese

Breakfast #2/Brunch (10:00 a.m.)
chocolate donut & a bear claw

Lunch (noon)
chicken salad sandwich
two servings of pasta salad
fruit

Dunch (4:30 p.m.)
(entire) box of macaroni and cheese
apple

Dinner (6:30 p.m.)
steak
rice
green salad

After Dinner Snack (9:00 p.m.)
four oatmeal cookies

After-After Dinner Snack (bedtime)
Cheetos

Now maybe it's just me, but aren't there about five real meals in there? And this just happened in the past two weeks! My wife acts like she's in training for the Nathan's hot dog eating contest, even though there's no way she'll be able to touch that little Japanese dude, she's still going to give it a shot!

My wife's doctor told her at the first doctor's visit, "Don't get obsessed about your weight. The average woman gains between 25 and 35 pounds during pregnancy. If you have a few months where you only gain two or three pounds, that's fine, but don't be surprised if there's one month when you gain 10. And that's normal, so don't sweat it." Well, that whole conversation makes sense after seeing the eating machine of a woman that my wife has become. Maybe this is just a good way to prepare for feeding three people.

Update-Month 9: It's been mentioned before, and it will probably be mentioned again, but I can't stress it enough: your significant other is going to lose 10-15 lbs with the delivery of the baby. You're not going to lose a thing. If you've been keeping pace with the missus during her eating binges that's all well and good, but just remember that you're not the one that's going to pop a baby out of that expanding midsection. I speak from experience ... six months into this thing I hadn't gained an ounce. Now, three months later I'm packing it on like I'm prepping for a winter with the Eskimos.

Chapter 4

Was That You?

Personal admonition here: I stink. Blame it on four years of college when I basically lived in funk-infested dorm rooms with other guys who had no cares about bodily odor (except Thursday to Saturday nights) or the general stench of a pizza box & stale beer filled room. Blame it on roommates who got joy from butter-cupping each other, leaving "damage" in parties and blaming it on one another, and generally living an unsanitary life filled with noxious fumes created from burps and farts. Blame it on the dining hall, too. For those of you that ate dining hall food on a daily basis you know that regularity was never an issue. Just a question of whether you had enough time to get from the cafeteria to the bathroom without losing some of lunch. I guess after a while, you kind of become numb to the stench. And that's probably preparation for pregnancy.

During pregnancy, your wife is going to become that college roommate that used to leave damage without claiming it, only there will probably just be two of you in the room ... unless she's lucky enough to have a dog to blame it on. My wife is not a smelly person by nature, and truthfully, she hasn't become too bad, but there are times when she emits odors that I could only associate with a rough night of drinking topped off with a six-egg, sausage and cheese omelet. And it's burps, too! For the first two months of the pregnancy, there wasn't a night that went by when she didn't sound like a member of a beer chugging team. "*Eeerp!* Excuse me." Jeez, honey, I thought you were cutting back on the onions!

So, what to do to prepare for this? Nothing. Let's face it. After the early stages of dating, you probably got real comfortable with your wife ... to the point where you started acting more like that college oaf than the smooth, romantic that you pretended to be for the first three months of courtship. And when you did start to return to your normal stinky self she didn't say much, if anything, to you about your funk. If she did get on your case about it, well, this still isn't the time to put it back on her. See, when your significant other is pregnant, a lot of what happens to her is not by her choice. Weight gain, random hair growth, emission of toxic gases, and so on. So, don't get on her case about her gas, it'll only make things worse. My advice to you? Do the same thing you do when she calls your name from upstairs to ask if you'll help her fold the laundry. Act like you didn't hear (smell) a thing.

Update: Month 5- The missus belts out burps like she was raised at a truck stop. Can happen before, during or after just about every meal, never smell bad, but are always audible, and usually just make me jump a little bit. I haven't heard belching like this since our college tailgate parties. Oh, and the random guttural noises that emanate from her like clockwork five minutes after dinner ... wow, that's something I should record and use to scare the bejesus out of the neighborhood kids at Halloween.

I've been told that this will continue throughout the remainder of the pregnancy, and aside from the lack of warning, I don't mind at all. In fact, it kind of gives me some idea of what it's like to live with me all the time. Equal justice, I guess.

Update: Month 7- I'm not completely sure about what just happened, and my wife's probably going to kill me for putting this in writing for all to see, but it has to be shared because it may happen to you.

We were walking into a grocery store after her 28-week check-up (which went fine, by the way, thanks for asking), and, remember how I told you that things happen without warning? Burps, hiccups, other toxic gases being dispelled from her body without notice for her or me? Yeah, well, when we got about 20 feet from the entrance, without warning, my wife sneezes. No biggie, right? Well, what would you think if I told you that she followed her sneeze up with a, "I just wet myself" comment?

"You wha?"

Are you kidding me?! A sneeze suddenly becomes wetting your pants? In month 8 will a burp bring on total loss of bowel control?

"First things first. Are you wearing white or khaki? No? Good. You should be safe for the moment. Second question: was it a gush or a trickle? In other words, can we complete the shopping trip, or do we need to hop in the car so that you can change your diaper, er, I mean your pants?"

What is happening to my wife?! I know she's got a lot going on in that region, but I'm only prepared to potty-train one person here, not two!

Chapter 5

The Onset of Narcolepsy

Maybe it's a female thing, I don't know. My sister has this innate ability to sleep anywhere, any time, under any condition. She's the perfect house guest to have around when you run out of beds, couches and floor space, and you're left with the stairs and the bathtub as sleeping options.

Well, before the pregnancy my wife could fall asleep pretty easily, but by no means could she just slip into la-la land at the drop of a hat. Now I don't know if it's some weird morphing that happens when women get pregnant or what, but I swear my wife suffered from narcolepsy for the first, ah, hell, she had it for the duration of the pregnancy. Maybe she became bear-like and needed to stock up on sleep before the baby was born; or maybe she was just completely wiped out from all the changes happening inside of her. Whatever it was, it was pretty freaky to witness. Falling asleep on the couch during the nightly news; catching some winks during the drive to work (don't worry, I was driving); nodding off mid-conversation.

"Hey, honey, what do you want to do for dinner?"

"Do you want to order out?"

"Sure,   where   do   you   want   to   ...
zzzzzzzzzzzzzzzzzzzzzzzzz"

"Honey? You with me?"

"Wha? Yeah, I'm here. Pizza. Let's do pizza."

Now don't get me wrong, there's an upside to this spontaneous slumber thing. We're talking total control over the remote every day and at all hours, because inevitably, even if you let her watch a home/person makeover show she'll be out before the first commercial comes on, and then it's back to ESPN.

Once narcolepsy kicks in, and it'll kick in pretty early in the pregnancy, it's not going anywhere for quite a while. We're talking until after the child can sleep through the night. And the worst part is that I hear it's contagious. Guys get it too, but that's only after the baby's born. So, just like you're enjoying the nine months of having a designated driver, enjoy your control of the remote, and your sleep, too. 'Cause once the critter comes along, you'll catch that narcolepsy bug, too.

Update: Month 8- Okay, the opposite is becoming true now. The missus can't sleep at all, and I'm not sure if it's because she's grown to epic proportions or what, but the fact is she doesn't sleep. Now from what I understand this is contradictory to what happens with a lot of women, mostly those who say that sleep in the final few weeks happens to get you prepared for the tiring first few months of parenthood.

Whatever the truth is, all I know is that my wife has become a Pillow Monster. Whether it's on the couch, or in bed, your wife, as the pregnancy moves along, will become more and more uncomfortable. And the more uncomfortable she is, the more pillows she'll want to surround herself with. By the ninth month, assuming you have a queen size bed, you'll definitely be sleeping on the couch because your wife will have collected just shy of three dozen pillows to replace the space that you used to occupy. There'll be a couple between her knees, one or two under her arms, of course one under her head, a few behind her back, and just to make it completely impossible for you to sleep in the same bed as her another five or six scattered around the rest of the bed.

My wife went so far as to get a body pillow. What's that you ask? Think "three pillows connected end to end that will officially replace you as what she wraps herself around at night". If only she'd had this problem when she wanted to cuddle.

Chapter 6

Riding the Roller Coaster of Mood Swings

Understand this: my wife is about the most even keeled person you could ever hope to meet. She's an eternal optimist bordering on being a real-life Suzie Sunshine. Me? Not quite as optimistic. Okay, so I'm yang to her yin. But, the point is, it's very difficult to get my wife down. She has the ability to let the bad stuff roll off her back, and the good stuff, boy, you've never seen happiness quite the way she expresses it; so genuine.

So, imagine my surprise, shock and awe, really, when I witnessed the first of what was to become many, many metamorphoses. Honestly, I don't remember what the situation was; the vividness of the experience was more focused on the speed at which my wife's mood was able to swing from one extreme to another. Happy to depressed. Despondent to perky. And back again. Unbelievable.

She could be bubbly and energetic, and then watch some random TV show with a piece about an old man who lost his driver's license because he'd run into a shopping cart and caused major fruit loss somewhere, and *bam*, cue the tears.

"What's the matter, honey? That guy is probably better off having someone else drive him places anyway."

"Yeah, but it's just so sad. I feel so bad for him."

Whatever.

Someone should time these things, seriously. Make it a new Olympic event or something. Think about it. Get seven or eight pregnant women from different countries competing against each other in the "Spontaneous Crying" event. Women from the Eastern bloc would never make it out of the prelims, and the U.S. women would probably sweep every time, what with their affinity for Dr. Phil & Oprah shows, but that's okay ... we need another event that we can win every time since men's basketball can't get it done. Another topic for another book.

Onward.

All I'm trying to tell you is that there are going to be times in the coming months where your significant other is going to burst into tears the way Buddhist monks used to burst into flames, and there more than likely will be no rhyme or reason why it's happening.

I can't believe this happened, but it did. I felt like I was trapped in one of those really, really bad 20-something movies where the woman wants the guy, but she's not hot enough for him, so she cries all the time to her best friend, until they decide to give the girl a makeover, and then *magically* she's the hottest thing going, and the guy and girl end up falling in love. You know those movies ... your wife's made you watch them more than once. It's okay to admit it. I won't tell anyone. Honest.

Anyway, I came home from work, and my wife was moping around not really telling me what was wrong. I didn't think that I'd done anything wrong, but I asked anyway.

"Honey, what's the matter? Did I do something to upset you?"

(cue the tears ... slow at first ... welling up in her eyes, filling like pools until one big fat drop bursts the eye-lid dam, and rolls over the top ... gently down her cheek)

"Nothing."

(more tears ... a steady stream running now, more like a small river than a creek)

"Are you sure? Did something happen that you want to tell me about?"

"No."

(bury the face in the pillow now ... more tears, and gentle sobbing)

"Sweetie. Something's bothering you. Otherwise you wouldn't be crying. Why don't you just tell me what's wrong?"

(uncontrollable sobbing now ... followed by ...)

"I" (sniff, sob) "don't" (sniff, sob) "know" (sniff, sob).

Oh crap. What do you do in that situation? There's only so much back rubbing, and "shhh"ing a guy can do before he just loses it, and says, "Get a grip! You don't even know why you're crying!"

Thankfully, I didn't get to that point. And if I did, I can safely assume that I'd be typing using a stick between my teeth to punch out the letters, because my wife would have broken every bone in my back-rubbing hands.

Reality checks are okay for the missus, you know, the "Honey, if you don't know why you're crying, why don't you try to relax and stop the tears? We'll watch some TV, maybe even TLC, and you can calm down a little bit. Can I get you some cookies?" But try not to go to the extreme, where you're calling her a ninny for crying at nothing, and making her feel like the private to your drill sergeant.

A little back stroking and soothing words can go a long way toward helping make the downswings that much more tolerable, and maybe even help shorten their duration. As for warning signs, and things that may set her off, I've compiled a list of some of the things that I noticed set my wife off, and my comments on whether it's reasonable to react the way she did or not:

1) Anything having to do with children in trouble, whether real or fictional. My take? Okay, this can be upsetting to just about anyone, no matter how heartless you are. Read a story about a local kid who lost his parents in a fire? Terrible tragedy.

Cue the tears. An after school special about a 16 year-old kid from Bel Air who has to drive an Audi to school instead of a Mercedes? Just doesn't cut it for me.

2) Just about anything that has to do with real-life tragedies, on the news, in the newspaper or magazines, on TV, etc. My take? Again, if it's real, it's hard not to tug at you a little bit. But uncontrollable sobbing about the middle-aged couple who lost their beach home in a hurricane, but are going to collect double that in insurance money? Not so much.

3) Weight loss stories. My take? God bless you if you can take off inordinate amounts of weight, whether through diet, surgery, or a combination of the two. But, you know what? I don't care how bad your genetics are, you had to eat like crazy to get that way. Personal success? You betcha. Worthy of tears? Doubtful. Gets the missus every time, though. Every god-blessed time.

4) Women who hardly gained weight/shed the pounds quickly during/after the birth of a child (or children). My take? I'd like to lynch the folks at *People*, *Us*, and just about every other weekly magazine that shows off the women of Hollywood during and after pregnancies. It's bad enough that our significant others espouse to look like skeletons, er, I mean, Lara Flynn Boyle, but why have covers with, "Gwyneth Paltrow is

7 ½ months pregnant ... and she's only gained 3 pounds!"?! That's below the belt.

5) Any fictional movie or TV show that has a happy, sappy ending. My take: Hardly ever is a TV show or movie worthy of tears (*Hoosiers* and *Field of Dreams* excluded), but any more, no matter how silly the premise, my wife cries at everything: comedy, drama, suspense, horror, I mean, when she lost it during *Cold Mountain*, that was pretty understandable ... classic love story with good acting, you know, obvious tissue material. Hell, they probably should give you Kleenex when you buy the ticket. But, reruns of *Miami Vice* on TNT?! Come on! When Tubbs got shot down for a date it was surprising to all of us, but there was no reason for tears!

Now, here's the difficult part of the story: these things don't go away. Mood swings last for the duration. No end in sight, my friend. In fact, once the baby's here, they may get worse! Figure, you have the same chemical imbalance going on, compounded by a baby sucking the life from you (and more things from your wife), and you've got yourself an at-home roller coaster. And just like all roller coasters there are good parts, bad parts, scary parts, unexpected parts, and adrenaline rushes. Expect all of these, though, because otherwise you may find yourself on a terrifying ride with no lap belt.

Chapter 7

Metamorphosis

This is a no-brainer, right? I mean, all guys know that when a woman gets pregnant, she gains weight, and that's that. Right? Wrong. A lot of women don't "show" for the first four or five months, and some don't even show then. For the purposes of this book, though, there's really only one physical change that you need to be totally aware of right now:

Boobs.

Your wife's boobs, no matter what size they were before, are going to get bigger. Some more than others, but all women get bigger breasts during pregnancy. And here, my friends, is the greatest catch-22 of all time. They're bigger, better and even more untouchable than they were before.

"Don't touch them, they're sore" will replace "Honey, I have a headache", or "I'm too tired, how about tomorrow?" as the most common good night phrase from your wife.

So why on earth is this happening? Why are men throughout the world being punished by this phenomenon? It's payback for the changes and the pain that women have to endure during the 9 months of pregnancy, and especially the actual birth. It's a daily reminder to men that women are the ones going through the hell of weight gain, morning sickness, constant discomfort and squeezing a seven-pound creature through a not-so-big opening.

So your wife is going to have enlarged boobs, and you're not going to be able to touch them. Think that's the worst part? Think again.

Update: Month 8- Before I let you get to the next chapter it's only fair for me to tell you that I was premature in saying that the only change you're going to need to worry about is boobs. That's probably going to be the change you'll notice first, and pay most attention to, but truth be told, your significant other is going to expand in a lot of places, some good, some not so good.

Actually, I've already covered the good. The rest of it, unless your wife is one of those women who has never really had an ass before, is not so good. I've witnessed some expansion in the hips, legs and butt areas, and hey, I'll be honest, I've expanded in those places, too. But now I'm told that her face may change, too, like her nose may get really wide, and her chin may grow little chins of their own. One of the strangest, though, is the belly button. The pregnant woman's belly button is like one of those turkey thermometers that pops when the cooking is finished. Yeah, your wife's belly button may pop out when the baby gets to a certain point in the brewing process. Pretty creepy, but a band-aid can hold that thing down.

Update: Month 9-Swelling. I thought that what had been happening for the past 8 months was swelling, but apparently that was just "normal weight gain". The official swelling has now begun, and her legs look like kielbasas. Best advice to cure it? Less salt, elevate the feet, and don't eat so damn much. Okay, that last part was just my own suggestion.

Chapter 8

S-E-X

Now this is the section that all mothers, fathers and in-laws need to skip. Especially mine. Seriously, for my comfort level and yours, just put the book down right now, or at least skip to the next chapter.

Okay, now that they've left the room, let's get on with it.

The thing with sex during pregnancy is that a lot of it depends on the couple. Some couples have sex like rabbits, and some couples (like everyone's parents and grandparents) only have sex the number of times it takes to make the number of children that are in your family. But, there are a lot of other factors that come into play here: how does your wife feel during those first few months when there's not much noticeable change to her physical appearance?; how do you feel knowing that a baby's growing inside her belly?; and, how was your sex life before she got pregnant?

Without going into too much detail I will tell you this: your sex life will change during pregnancy. For some, it will change dramatically, and for others, not so much. Sometimes the changes happen right off the bat, and other times they evolve slowly. But no matter what, there will be change.

Let's just look at the physical limitations that are evolving here. Your significant other is gaining quite a bit of weight in one particular area, and that weight-gain area can limit where you are, my friend. So, right off the bat, you're going to have to mix things up a little bit. Get a little creative. Don't invest in a front-end loader or anything, but missionary just won't cut it after a while.

Then there's the whole comfort level factor. For one, your wife may be feeling sick for a good portion of those first months, and sex will probably be the last thing on her mind (if it wasn't already). Then there's the comfort level (or lack of) that she may feel considering the huge changes that she's going through. Don't forget, unlike most guys, who generally don't mind when their six pack turns into a mound of fleshy dough, women are very concerned with their physical appearance, and even though lots of people will coo at how cute your wife gets during her pregnancy, that flattery isn't going to help you get her to the bedroom. If the missus feels like crap because she's starting to get stretch marks, or because she's gaining weight in a place she's never carried any extra before, well, you better just understand that her self-esteem is probably not going to be where it needs to be to get down and dirty. Flowers and cooking dinner may help, but remember that for a lot of women the way they feel physically about themselves can play a huge part in whether you're going to rock and roll.

Now, it's been said that for some women, pregnancy increases their sexual appetite, and for others, it decreases the appetite for lovin'. I can only speak to how my wife was during her pregnancy … and let's just say that she didn't have much of an appetite. And even on those occasions when she was hungry things didn't always work out as planned.

On our 1st wedding anniversary we spent a long weekend in NYC doing the touristy things that folks do: shopping, getting ignored by taxis, paying three times as much as any person should for a decent meal, you know, the usual. And in typical New York fashion the hotel where we stayed, while very modern and cool, did not have very spacious accommodations. Well, we weren't going to let cramped quarters spoil our fun, or so we thought. The missus and her 7th month pregnant belly barely fit in the shower (we had to grease the sides with butter just to get her in and out), so that was out of the question, and the bed was a glorified single, so the comfort level wasn't too high there, either. And when you rule out the shower and the bed, you're basically left with the floor. Well, you try to convince a 7 months pregnant woman to lie down on the hardwood floor for some passion. You've got a better shot of getting her to skip a meal than lie down for that.

Overall, sex during the pregnancy, just like sex pre-pregnancy, is totally dependent on the couple. Some of you folks are trying to set land and speed records, and others more closely resemble the giant sloth exhibit at the zoo. Regardless, just be prepared for some changes in the future. Some for the better, and well, some that require you to find a hobby to occupy your new found free time, like bb stacking or knitting.

Chapter 9

Check Ups

Ugh.

No one likes to go to doctor's appointments, but for some reason, when your significant other is pregnant, she wants you to suffer through the god-blessed event once every month for 7 months. What happens in months 8 and 9, you ask? Oh, well in month 8 you get to go twice a month, and in month 9 it's once a week! Yeah, sitting in a waiting room for forty-five minutes reading the latest articles from breastandbelly.com sounds like loads of fun, doesn't it. I only wish I was kidding about that title ... it's a real website. Trust me here.

So, even though you know that your wife is pregnant, it's good to be supportive, and if you can afford to take part of the day off of work, and even if you can't, she's going to ask you to go. To every single appointment. It's true that after month one and two, it's pretty much straight forward, check the blood pressure, check the weight, check the baby's heartbeat type of stuff, but your wife's going to want you to be there. For some reason, she thinks you'll enjoy the forty-five minute wait, interrupted midway by one of the office people asking your wife to pee in a cup. Then, once you do get to go to Holding Tank #2 (the waiting area is Holding Tank #1), you're subjected to less open space, fewer windows, if there are even windows at all, and totally outdated magazines, like the issue of Parenting Magazine with Florence Henderson on the cover. I'll never forget one of the first visits to HT2, when my wife was devouring one of those magazines (not literally, although if you'd given her some mayo, she may have tried to), and I couldn't force myself to read Cat in the Hat, so I started reading the posters on the wall. You know, the "How to Properly Massage Your Newborn" posters. I was actually reading about this stuff.

My advice to you: bring a book, or a Gameboy, or something. Don't know that I'd go the route of "totally disinterested dad" by bringing an iPod, or a CD player, but if that's all you have available, do it. You'll need something to pass the time. Why aren't you going to talk with your wife? Because if she's like 93.4% of women, she'll want to talk to you about the other people in the waiting room.

"Do you think she's pregnant?" or "How far along do you think she is?" or "Boy, check her out. She could go at any minute!"

Appointment #3 was absolutely amazing, though.

Understand that up until this point, my wife had only been to two appointments, and aside from being told that she can't drink alcohol, and that she was going to need to get ten tubes of blood taken for tests to be run, there wasn't much new information from the doctor. So, since I knew there wasn't going to be an ultrasound given, I figured this appointment would be more of the same: blood pressure & weight check; "How're you feeling?" from the nurse or doctor, "Pretty good" from my wife; you know, the usual.

Not this check-up, though. I should've known something funky was going to happen when the doctor asks my wife to take off her shirt, and then the doc breaks out a tube of clear gel and squeezes it all over my wife's stomach ... nasty, I know. Then she takes out this thing that looks like one of those paddles hospitals have to kick-start a heart when it's stopped beating. Thankfully, the doctor wasn't kick-starting any hearts. But the paddle-thing did have something to do with a heart. Listening to a heart ... my baby's heart! It sounded like a little hummingbird fluttering inside of my wife's stomach! That was easily the coolest thing that I've ever heard. Trust me on this one: when you hear a heartbeat that is definitely not your significant other's emanating from the middle of her stomach it will rock your world. Hell, it rocked mine so much I agreed to let my wife buy an at-home Doppler thingee so that she can check the baby's heartbeat all the time. And no, the novelty of hearing that never wears off.

(Un)fortunately, the "heartbeat-for-the-first-time" visit is the pinnacle of doctor's visits (aside from the ultrasound), and barring any complications the doctor's visits become pretty routine, with some time spent in HT 1, then a move to HT 2, and finally a quick 74 second visit from the doctor who asks, "How are you feeling?", followed by, "Well, your blood pressure & weight look good. The baby seems to be doing fine, so I'll see you in about four weeks."

And just like that, your wife's doctor has made another $200, and you've spent over an hour reading back issues of women's magazines. So it goes.

Update: Month 8- Okay, these things are getting a little out of control. We're starting to go twice a month now, and apparently, we're going to go once a week for the last month. Do you realize how much PS2 time is being wasted on these things? Granted, if you're lucky enough to get out of work early to go to these things, all the better, but chances are your significant other has planned these appointments for right after work so the only thing you're missing is the post-work beverage of your choice, and the beginning of four consecutive hours of SportsCenter or your fifth season of Madden. Either way, you're missing out on something.

Okay, okay, how can I be such an insensitive bastard about these doctor's appointments? Call it too much time spent in HT 1 & 2, or just the fact that I'm the poster-child for adult ADD, whatever the case is these appointments are a nice way to make sure that everything's a-okay with the little guy. But the steadily increasing number of appointments just as you're beginning to realize how precious your "young with no commitments" time is? It's a little tough to swallow ... especially since I'm missing SportsCenter.

Chapter 10

War Stories

Every woman your wife talks to is going to have a story, if not seven or eight about their experience with pregnancy. These first-hand stories are generally told in relation to whatever stage your wife happens to be in at the time. If your wife just found out she's pregnant, she'll hear the "I-couldn't-keep-anything-down-for-three-months" stories. And if she's a little further along, it'll be the "well, I-blew-up-like-a-whale" stories, or worse, the "I-only-gained-11-pounds" stories". But the worst stories, by far, are the late in the pregnancy horror stories that will make your wife launch out of bed in the middle of the night sweating profusely and beating you with a pillow for "doing this to her". Yes, the labor stories are priceless.

As my wife got closer to actually giving birth, these stories began to sink in more and more, and she developed a strange fascination with the size of my cranium, her cranium, and the size of all of our family members' craniums, too. I guess that would be the most intimidating part of the birth for a woman, and your wife will probably sweat this too. I mean, think about it, a human skull is going to be pushed through a not-so-big opening, certainly not human head size, anyway, and your significant other is the one that has to bear this burden. So, if you're one of those people who has an inordinately large noggin', you'd better start apologizing right now.

I've been witness to stories about 30+ hours of labor, and 45 minute deliveries. These pretty much cancel each other out because they're the extremes. The ones that really register with women are the ones that keep repeating themselves over and over and over again. Like, "I've never been in so much pain before in my life", and "I wanted to quit until they gave me the epidural (pain medication), and then everything was a-okay", and "I literally couldn't walk for a couple of days". These are the ones that register the most. The extreme cases fall by the wayside, and your wife will focus mostly on these things:

1) excruciating pain
2) epidural
3) excruciating pain

Truth be told, though, you have no idea how bad this is going to be, and even after the fact, you won't know. Your spouse may inflict some sort of pain on you during the delivery, which I'm told is pretty common, but it won't even begin to compare to what she's experiencing. Rumor has it that giving birth for a woman is comparable to urinating a golf ball for a man. Think about that for a second: a golf ball. One more time: a golf ball. That thing has no business coming out of that small of an opening. None. So, never, ever, ever, ever, ever, ever, ever say anything about the pain that your wife will experience, because I don't know anyone out there who'd be able to handle peeing a golf ball.

Update: Month 8 ½- Fair warning: Do not, unless you want to spend the last two weeks of the pregnancy drying tears and paying for therapy, let your wife read internet stories about childbirth. My wife searched the web for stories about induction (looks like the little sucker's too warm and cozy to come out on his own), and "stumbled" on a page of stories submitted by mothers about their childbirth experience. My wife sent a couple of these bad boys my way, and let me tell you, I'd rather read a Stephen King short story than some of the things these women wrote. I swear, she must have been reading these things on hellishdeliverystories.com. The kicker? At the end of every one of the stories the author tried to be cutesy about how it was all worth it because "little Austin" was here and healthy, or whatever. Give me a break! After you detail the amount of blood you lost, the intense pain you felt, and the tears you shed you're going to try to soften the blow by spitting out one sentence about the joy you felt at the end of 16 hours of intense labor? If ever there was a need for internet censoring this is it. No close-to-full-term pregnant woman should be allowed to read something like that ... and no man should have to dry eyes and listen to his fear-stricken woman because of some bonehead who felt compelled to share her hellish experience on the internet.

Chapter 11

How Much Will This Cost?

If you're anything like my wife and me, pre-pregnancy, a good chunk of your weekly change was spent on going out & throwing back a few drinks, five or six nights a week. Well, the little one on the way certainly has changed that lifestyle, now hasn't it? Okay, so you've got a built-in DD for nine months, but chances are your wife's not going to want to hang out in the same haunts that you frequented pre-pregnancy. And even if she does, drinking alone isn't nearly as much fun, and if it is, there are a couple of organizations you may want to call to "get help".

So, how is the little one going to change your monthly expenses and your long-term planning ("'Long-term planning? What's that?'")? Well, babies are expensive, and your beer buys are going to be replaced by diapers, formula, bottles, bibs, onesies (the little outfits your newborn will spend most of his time in), Dreft (special baby laundry detergent), and pacifiers. Yes, you'll need to buy a crib, a stroller, a dresser, cute little toys, and all that other crap that's going to pile up where you used to keep your decade old collection of Sports Illustrated, but that's the way parenthood works. And, if you've got really cool friends and family (read: generous and loaded), you may be able to knock some of this stuff out with a baby shower. Hopefully, there's someone on your wife's side that will plan these events so that you don't have to completely go the charity route and start begging people for stuff.

Food

"Another mouth to feed" is one thing you probably heard on sitcoms growing up every time a show had the mom telling the dad, "Honey, I'm pregnant." You remember those shows; they were always promo'ed as "Tonight, on a very special episode of (fill in random 80s sitcom) ...". Then, invariably the show jumped the shark, and was off the air within a season or so. Sam on Diff'rent Strokes, Oliver on the Brady Bunch, Luke on Growing Pains, Scrappy on Scooby Doo, you know.

So, why do 80s shows jumping the shark have anything to do with your child? Well, it's that misconception that "another mouth to feed" is going to force you to take a second job as a Slushee server in an all-night convenience store. You see, it is another mouth to feed, but it's a really small mouth. And that mouth is pretty much in proportion to the size of its stomach, which means the baby won't eat too much. In fact, your baby's stomach is about the size of a marble ... no, not one from Hungry, Hungry Hippos, the bigger kind, but still, it's a marble for God's sake! Plus, if your wife is dead-set on breast-feeding, it's like having a built-in fridge right there in your wife's boobs! And best of all, it's free!

Chances are, your wife will breastfeed part of the time, and then want the baby to switch to formula at some point after she complains about how raw and sore her nipples are, and before the child's ready to move on to solid foods. Unless your wife is going to be one of those creepy people you see in the mall who breastfeeds their 6 year-old. If that's your wife you'd better start saving for your child's psychiatry visits right now.

But if your wife is like most she'll try breast feeding, do it for a while, and then decide to make the switch to more solid foods. Even when this happens the expense isn't going to be that great. Several jars of baby food ought to last a few days, and those things are pennies a piece. It's not like your child's going to start ordering the surf-and-turf at 6 months. So, don't sweat the increased number of "mouths to feed" ... until your child hits 12, then you can really worry. Until then, though, you're safe.

So what's the cost like? Well, a large powdered formula can, which lasts anywhere from 2-3 weeks depending on how much your child eats, how much your wife breastfeeds, etc., will cost about $25. If you buy the ready-to-eat stuff (you have to add water to the powder) than it'll be more ... a lot more. Save your money, use your water, and buy the powder. Oh, and look for it at wholesale places (BJ's, Price Club, Costco, etc.) if you're trying to find it at a better price.

Diapers and Clothes

Here's where your money's going to be spent. Oh sure, that other stuff (food, furniture, toys) is going to cost some cash, too, but as far as ongoing expense, diapers and clothes is where it's at. You see, you'll be changing those diapers, 10, 15, 20 times a day. Sometimes you won't even get the diaper all the way on the baby, and the fountain will have sprung again, which means, yes, you have to put on another diaper. For some guys the actual changing of the diapers is a more daunting task than paying for them. And paying for them is not too easy. It's not that diapers are expensive all by themselves so much as it is that you're going to need so many of them! And since your baby will be growing faster than Barry Bonds head (ego and actual noggin), you're going to need to buy diapers in different sizes all the time. Your best bet for diapers is a wholesale place, like BJs, Sam's Club or Costco ... buying diapers in bulk is a helluva lot more economical than ketchup, because you'll use every one of them.

The same goes for clothes. Depending on the amount of clothing you have for your child, and how fast the baby grows, don't be surprised if there are some clothes that the baby only wears once before outgrowing them. Don't sweat it. Your wife probably has ten pairs of shoes that she's never worn hiding under the bed. And if you think I'm wrong, think again. Women buy shoes the way we buy power tools. At least our impulse buys are useful.

Onesies are those cute little outfits that babies wear and you can't get enough of them. Honestly, there'll be times when your baby pees through one, pees on the next one as you're putting it on, and then spits up as soon as you get the third one fastened. So you're on to your fourth onesie in under a minute. Having twenty-five or thirty of these things makes sense. Trust me.

And cute outfits? Yeah, they're fun to dress your child in but it's not the worst thing in the world to wear hand-me-downs. Or buy some clothes at Marshall's or TJ Maxx.

All in all, the increased spending isn't too, too bad. If you're not above clipping coupons and borrowing stuff (bassinette, crib, etc.) then you may not even notice much of a change at all. And if your alcohol consumption is still under what it was pre-baby than you may have actually saved yourself a few bucks. It's never too early to start saving for college.

Chapter 12

Shopping

The single word above this sentence sends shivers up 99.9995% of all men's spines. And the 0.0005% of men who say they don't mind shopping are lying.

Well, if you just found out that your wife is pregnant you are totally hosed. It doesn't matter how much she shopped pre-pregnancy, she's going to shop a lot more. Unless your wife lives at the mall, and by "lives at the mall" I mean that quite literally, she will be spending more time "just picking up a few things" than she ever did in the past.

Case in point: my wife is not a big shopper by nature ... I mean, when she shops, she tries very hard to break the bank, but she usually makes shopping for clothes/furniture/stuff for the house a semi-annual thing, so I can tolerate that. With this pregnancy, though, it became one production after another! "We need furniture for the baby", "We need clothes for the baby", "We need children's books", "We need toys", "We need a stroller, a car seat, a breast pump (dear God, please don't even ask), a rocking chair, a changing table, new paint for the room, a new carpet, ..." and the list goes on. And that's just for the baby. Then there's the whole, "Well, I'm going to need a whole new wardrobe" speech she laid on me. Okay, I can understand that you're going to be packing on the pounds with this baby, but is there any need to buy every "cute little maternity" piece of clothing you find? My wife's got spring, summer, fall and winter maternity clothes, and she was only showing for the last month of summer and all of the fall ... so why all the clothes? Because pregnancy heightens a woman's shopping desire.

It seriously doesn't matter where your significant other goes, she'll find something to buy that she can justify with, "But it'll be good for the baby", or "But I need it because I'm pregnant", and you just have to sit there and take it, because you're not the one carrying the little critter in your belly. A quick trip to the drug store to pick up panty hose will now cost you $63.48 because she found a cute bottle and pacifier set in a color that matches the baby's room, plus they were having a sale on diapers, and you can never have too many diapers, plus she snagged four candy bars at the checkout because, well, because she can, because she's pregnant.

If you're lucky some of your friends or family have had kids before you, and your wife can borrow some of the maternity clothes from them. If not, though, you could be completely screwed trying to re-stock your wife's closet with a completely new wardrobe. The good thing is, just like with regular sized people clothes, the price ranges vary. The bad thing is that women have an internal tracking system that only allows them to shop in the most exclusive stores which basically forces you to make a choice: give in to letting her buy $140 jeans (thus causing you to eat Ramen noodles for dinner for the next week); or tell her "No", and face the wrath of the mood-swinging maniac that you used to call your wife. So, either way, you're hosed.

My suggestion to you? ... outlet shopping. I was fortunate enough to find a maternity clothes outlet, and I let my wife go nuts in the place while I was looking at stereo equipment in another store. We still dropped a good amount of money, but it was probably half of what we would have spent on the same stuff if we'd been at a non-outlet store. Plus, I picked up a sweet pair of speakers for the house. Win-win situation.

Chapter 13

Birthing Class

Note the name of the chapter. The working title was "Lamaze class, and all the stupid crap that you waste time learning about but will never use", but that was too long. Plus, my wife corrected me. It's birthing class, not Lamaze class. Big difference. What's the difference you ask? Hell if I know. If you find out, let me know because I'd love to hear it.

Our particular class was not specifically geared just toward breathing (that's Lamaze), but instead the class covered the basics of being a parent: everything from getting your pregnant spouse to the hospital to what the room where the delivery is going to happen looks like, to how to swaddle your baby and give it a bath. Oh, and they covered breathing, too, but let's be honest, if you're wife can't breath she wouldn't be here, and once those contractions start, most of that stuff is going to fly out the window anyway.

This class did subject the group to more than one video of "an actual birth". I say that because those shows that have births always give fair warning by saying something ridiculous like, "What you are about to see is an actual birth". Thanks for that update from the department of the obvious, Tonto. When you see a woman squeezing the life out the person standing next to them, and screaming shouts of pain reserved for war, you'll know it's "an actual birth", thank you very much.

The videos weren't too bad, and they did prep you for the kind of things you don't usually think about, like just how much blood and "stuff" (that's a medical term) is going to ooze, or pour, out of your wife. Oh, they did leave one thing out, though, that was brought up in the class:

Pooping.

It all makes sense, really, when you think about it, what with all that pushing down there. All that grunting and straining and forcing something out shouldn't surprise you at all if something else comes out before the baby. Don't worry about it, most women do it, and the docs and nurses have definitely seen it before, so if it does happen, your wife's not a freak, she's just normal. And if it does happen, don't be a jerk and bring it up after the fact. But if she decides to bring it up first, it's okay to share a laugh about it, because it is kind of funny, in that 4th grade, laugh at poop jokes sort of way.

Overall the class was a good way for the wife to meet some other large-and-in-charge women who were in the same boat as her (a very sturdy boat, I might add), and getting ready to burst. Plus, I did learn some things that I didn't know before, like swaddling, how to give the baby a bath, and just how much blood loss is involved during childbirth. Good times.

Chapter 14

Nesting

Major point to consider: leaving your home without your wife for any length of time during her pregnancy may result in your significant other completely re-designing your house, especially the baby's room, which will in turn leave you submerged in more debt than dating her did.

Case in point: I agreed to do a bike tour with my father and a bunch of other people in Colorado and New Mexico (the old one is just too dirty) for about a week and a half at the midpoint of her pregnancy. Now realize, I agreed to do this before we found out she was pregnant, and even after we found out, we both agreed that it would be fine because she wasn't far enough along to worry about too much. So, no worries for either of us, right? Ha!

The first three days I was away my wife spent over $1,000. That's not a type-o.

Yeah, so I cut the trip a little short, came home, confiscated the cards and locked her in a closet.

Okay, so that's not entirely true, but the damage certainly is. Don't get me wrong, the room(s) look terrific, which I'm sure will last about 8 minutes after we bring the baby home, since all babies do is sleep, eat, poop and pee, but for the time being, she's done a masterful job of pulling a Martha Stewart (pre-conviction, that is).

So what's this nesting thing that everyone talks about? Well, in a nutshell it's the only way to get your house to be absolutely spotless without hiring a team of professional cleaners. In the days leading up to the due date your significant other will start doing things that you never imagined she would ever do, like scrubbing the kitchen floor on her hands and knees, cleaning around the toilet with a toothbrush (hopefully not yours), and vacuuming multiple times day. It's like she's preparing for some white-glove test that's never going to happen. And if the house starts to get dirty again, she does it all over ... it's awesome on so many levels. It means that your house looks more like a museum than a home, plus it gives you more time to play PS2 before the baby comes. And, it keeps your wife from buying those "oh-so-cute" outfits that you know she would be buying if she was out of the house.

Nesting is something that comes out of nowhere and I have a feeling that it will never be seen or heard from until all this happens again ... kind of like Ralph Nader.

Chapter 15

Random Thoughts That Aren't Worthy of a Whole Chapter, But Are Definitely Worth Mentioning

- TLC- Dear god, why do women flock to this TV channel like rednecks to a NASCAR race? All this channel does is freak women out! Think about it, people it's television, you know, entertainment? So, do you really think they're going to make a thirty minute television show about a totally and completely normal pregnancy and birth?! If your wife wasn't a TLC watcher before the pregnancy, she will be now. The show is "A Baby Story", and unless you are a total glutton for punishment you'll find something else to do while this is on. Otherwise, you're going to spend 60 minutes (two 30-minute episodes usually play back-to-back) watching your significant other getting progressively more teary-eyed until she finally bursts into tears at the sight of the baby being delivered ... and yes, they show it. So, if I were you, I'd find something to do while the show is on, yard work, painting, reorganizing canned goods, whatever, just make sure you avoid the tube during "A Baby Story". And God bless you when they have A Baby Story marathon weekend.

- Random Hair Growth and the Onset of Acne-
  Well, it pretty much boils down to that. But
  just to prepare you, your wife's going to have
  a random hair or three pop out of places where
  they shouldn't ... like her chin! Thankfully, it
  hasn't happened to my wife, but let me tell you, if
  she ends up looking anything like one of our old
  librarians, she may as well invest in Gillette. The
  zits may not be anything new for your significant
  other, but if they are, just grab some Oxy, and let
  her go to town ... they probably won't be that bad,
  but it's just one more reason to be happy that it's
  her and not you. Can you imagine if you had to
  hear,

  "Gee, (insert your name here), are you ready for
  this morning's board meeting, or do you want to
  pop that nasty whitehead on your nose before we
  go in?"

- Clumsiness- This is another "relative" thing
  where you might be used to a clumsy wife, but
  if you're not, this is probably just preparation
  for having children around the house. My wife,
  who's as graceful as a swan, but clumsy as all hell,
  once spilled three glasses of water from the same
  table all in the same day. Granted, this is the same
  woman who once got into an accident with the
  same parked car twice ... in one day.

Regardless, though, she's going to have a few accidents
around the house, and may even add tripping to her
repertoire. My wife's tripped up stairs, down stairs, and

on level ground, and that was before she got pregnant, so needless to say, we've invested in lots of disposable dishes, and I've thought about just wrapping her completely in bubble wrap to prevent injury.

- Memory Loss- I forgot what I was going to write here. No, wait a minute, that's her, not me.

Seriously, though, my wife has completely lost her short-term memory. And it's not just ignoring me when I ask her to grab another plate of nachos from the kitchen. I sincerely believe that parts of her brain have been sucked out by our baby, and may never be returned. This started in the early going and has only gotten worse. Maybe I should start recording our conversations so that I can prove to her that, yes, we really did talk about how she'd change all diapers and do all midnight feedings if I promised to play with the baby during reasonable daylight hours.

Update: Month 8- On the morning drive to work one morning I innocently asked my wife what she was drinking. Her response sums up this ailment of pregnant women.

"It's cran-something, apple or grape, juice with ginko-balboa, or ginko-bloba, or, oh I don't remember what it is. Anyway, it's good for my memory."

Yup. That about sums it up.

- What are you having?- Well, hopefully it's a baby, but the question is, do you want to find out the baby's gender before the birth? My answer, as a practical person who plans things more often than not: Of course. How else are you going to know whether to paint the nursery like a fairy princess castle or the inside of Notre Dame Stadium. But, on the advice of our parents, but especially my father-in-law, we opted not to find out. Sure, this may put a kink in some of the planning, and now you may have to wait before you buy the pink or blue blankie for baby, but as it was posed to me, There are so few *good* surprises in your adult life, wouldn't this be the best one of all? And my answer to that is, yes, this will be the best surprise of all, and waiting just makes it that much cooler.

- Choosing Baby Names- Oh boy (or girl), this is a tough one. Do you offend your parents by naming the child after her family, do you offend her parents by naming the child after your family, or do you offend everyone by naming the child after Ashton Kutcher? There's nothing more personal than choosing your child's name, so there's not a whole lot of good advice to provide here, but there are a couple of rules you can follow, though. First of all, how does the name sound when you yell it ... you know, like when you're really, really mad and you're screaming up the stairs for that child to get his ass downstairs. If it works for that, that's good. Second, don't pick a trendy name that sounds really cool to you because no one else will ever pick that name, because one of two things will happen: either the child will truly be the only person in the world with that name, and you'll be paying therapist bills for the first twenty years of his life; or, that really cool, totally unique name that no one else has will be shared by 6 other kids in the child's 1st grade class, and he'll be called by a number instead of a name. "Cooper #4, it's your turn at the water fountain". How miserable.

- Social Scene- Very cool at the beginning. Not so cool toward the end. We're lucky enough to live in a state where smoking at places where food is served is illegal ("You're under arrest ... for smoking"). Anyway, for the first months of the pregnancy, when the missus wasn't showing, or wasn't showing very much, she was the ultimate designated driver, and she even seemed to have a good time, or at least pretended to have a good time. In the later months, though, when you're bringing your "big-as-a-house" wife into a bar for a few cold ones, well, the stares get a little uncomfortable. Plus, she's probably miserable and complaining about something, "My feet hurt" "People are staring at me" "I'm tired of watching other people drink" "I'm missing TLC", and everything else that goes along with it. Best idea? After you reach month 7 or so, know that Friday and Saturday nights will probably be spent at your house or apartment, ordering in and renting a movie. It's more comfortable for all parties involved, and just think of all the money you'll save on beer.

- Feedings- Now here's a question for the new father whose wife is breast-feeding: why do we have to get up when the baby cries in the middle of the night? I mean, honestly, the missus should have the feedings covered with boob breakfast, lactation lunch and d-cup dinner, so what role do we play here? Well, if you're a good human being you'll gladly assist your wife in this process at least part of the time. For feedings you'll use milk that's been pumped by your wife (story for another book), or formula, which, by the way, is priced very similarly to gold.

Chapter 16

Thar She Blows!

"It's time."

Those two words are all it took to shake me from a slumber, sit up out of bed and get me to break out the stopwatch. When your wife utters those words, or something similar, a chemical reaction will happen in your body that will make everything seem like a scene out of the Matrix where your whole life goes into slo-mo. The ticking of the clock while you're timing her contractions is worse than waiting for the popcorn to finish popping in the microwave. You want the contractions to come faster, but you want them to slow down all at the same time. And I'm afraid to tell you that, if it's the real deal, those puppies aren't slowing down.

Now there are several stages of labor, many of which I was unaware of before they were presented to me up close and personal by the missus. It's not uncommon to see some of these come in quick succession, or even happen at the same time, but regardless of how they happen during the birth of your child you will see all of these things.

The first stage is excitement. This one's easy enough. Your wife is excited to have finally started labor, and all you have to do in the early going is time those contractions.

Depending on your circumstances (read: if your wife's not in too much pain) you can resume normal activities (read: watching ESPN or playing video games). The early going here can last for quite a while, so don't expect junior to be in your arms before the end of the Simpsons. Until those contractions are 5 minute apart for at least an hour, chances are, your wife's doctor won't want her admitted to the hospital yet. So, you may as well get comfortable and just chill.

Now, once those contractions are five minutes apart consistently, you're on your way to becoming a daddy. So, hopefully your wife has her bag(s) packed and you've got the car gassed up. If you're reading this chapter as this is happening to your wife, put the book down and tend to her. If you're reading this ahead of time, and your wife doesn't have her bag packed, and your car is running on empty you'll need to take care of those not-so-minor details before you go forward.

Now that those things are taken care of you're ready to head to the hospital. Don't forget your wife, since she's going to play a pretty important role in this whole birth-of-your-child thing.

At this point, the excitement should still be there, with a little bit of fear mixed in, and that's normal. Just remember, your significant other is probably a lot more scared than you are, so try to keep your game face on ... plus, it can't hurt to score points by playing the part of the sensitive, caring husband. So, after you get to the hospital and check in the next phase should kick in ... fear.

Fear comes about when a person finds himself in a position where he's got no previous history and has no idea what is about to happen. That's where you'll find yourself after check-in to the hospital. Nurses will hook your wife up to an IV with some fluids, she may or may not want to lie down, and until the doctor comes in to pay a visit, there's not a whole lot you can do except sit and wait. This time that you and your spouse spend together is whatever you make it. You may decide to bring cards and play some poker, or maybe bring books or magazines (magazines with lots of pictures are a good distraction, since her focus and attention span can be measured in milliseconds during this time ... not a good time to pick up the latest Clancy novel).

Like I've said throughout this book, every woman is different so your significant other may want you in the room the whole time, or she may banish you to the waiting room. She may want you to talk with her, or she may want you to occupy yourself with a hobby (here's where that bb stacking comes in handy). She may want you to hold her hand during the contractions, or she may want to punch you during every one. It really just depends on her, and there's no way to gauge it before it starts happening, and by then it's too late to do anything about it. And don't think that just because your wife is one way in normal life that it's going to translate to the delivery room. She may be a shy, sweet little thing normally, but during labor she may pull your hair out, curse your name and threaten to cut off your bait and tackle. It's the hormones, fellas, it's all the hormones.

Once the doc's done an examination and determined how far along your wife is, that will really help determine how long you've got. Nothing's written in stone, but it seems to me that once labor begins for real (yes, there's such thing as false labor ... think of it as the practice right before the big game), the dilation goes about 1 cm per hour to hour-and-a-half. Now, if you don't already know, dilation gets to about 10 cm before the baby comes out ... do NOT break out a ruler and see how big 10 cm is because it will only creep you out and scare you out of doing this again.

So, if your doc comes in and tells you that your wife is about 5 cm, chances are, you've got a few hours left. And if you're this far along, chances are your wife is either beating you with every contraction, or she's on drugs.

Yes, your spouse will be on drugs ... magical, wonderful, mind (and body) numbing drugs during this ride. An epidural is highly recommended (no, dads, you don't get one too), and helps to reduce the pain of the contractions. Epidurals are tricky devils though because they can slow down contractions, and if they're given too early, they may wear off before the really difficult part of labor begins. And, if the missus is too far along the doctor may not give an epidural at all because that can slow down the natural flow of things (pun intended).

Side story: during my wife's labor we had to spend the night at the hospital because she was being induced. I was allowed to stay with her but I was banished (by the nurses, not my wife) to a wee little window seat for the night. Imagine my horror when I was awakened by screams of pain from the other side of the wall at 3:45 a.m.

Well, as it turns out the woman next door was admitted at 8 cm dilated (put your ruler away), and the doctor had determined that it was too late in the game to give her an epidural, so she was basically S.O.L. Well, the screams only lasted for another hour or so, the lady ended up having a healthy baby, and aside from scaring the holy hell out of everyone on the floor everything worked out just fine. But the lesson for all of you at home is this: make sure that your wife takes the drugs.

So, where was I? Oh yeah, about 5 cm dilated and hopped up on drugs (her, not me). Now this is the part of the labor where things start to get a little more exciting. The doctor is checking up on your wife more; there seems to be more eagerness from nurses coming in and out of the room; and your wife may begin to feel those contractions again. During the latter part of the labor your spouse may begin to hate you. Seriously. With all those hormones rushing through her body, plus the fear that's going through her brain and the unknown in front of her, she's got to take out her aggression on someone, and it will undoubtedly be you. And that's okay. Let it happen. She won't remember it the next day, and if you're a good partner, you'll just sit there and take it because she's doing 99.9% of the work in all this.

Now, once the delivery process starts, if your doctor is worth his/her salt, they're going to walk you through what's happening. And if you're a smart man you'll let the doctor do her thing, and you'll keep your head up near your wife's. God knows the doctor doesn't need two patients on their backs, and believe me, you may want to pass out if you catch a glimpse (and whiff) of what's going on down below.

This is not a time for candid camera or picture pages. You can videotape all you want, but my suggestion is that your opening shot be of your newborn, not the grunting and groaning of your wife to get there.

So, like I was saying, your doctor will hopefully be giving you a play-by-play of what's happening in the nether regions, if for no other reason than to motivate your wife to stick with it and push when she's supposed to. You'll hear something like, "I see the head", followed by "The head's out, and ..." dramatic pause ... "It's a ...".

And when you hear those words, well, I won't spoil that, but if you're unaffected by the sound of those words, and the first cry of your newborn then you're a cold, cold bastard.

All I can tell you is that you will probably get a little misty-eyed when it happens, and there's nothing wrong with that. Let it go, man, it's the coolest time in your life. And don't forget to hug and kiss your wife, too, because that little baby wouldn't be here without all her hard work.

And after you thank your wife and tell her that you love her, go enjoy your baby.

Chapter 17

I'm Doing Fine, Thanks for Asking

So you have a baby now. Easily the best moment of your life, right? Once you become a father everything will change, including how people look at you. If they even look at you at all.

If it hasn't started happening already everyone you know will begin asking you, in this order, "How's the baby?", and then "And how's your wife feeling?", and then ... and then ... that's it. No, "And how are you doing with all this?", or "And you look great, but are you getting enough sleep?", or even "And I hope you're doing well, too." It's just "How's the baby?" and "How's your wife feeling?" and nothing else.

You see, you were semi-important before the baby came, what with your midnight runs to the grocery store and your foot rubs for the missus, and whatnot. But now that the little one has arrived? You can exit stage left, and we'll call you when we need you. Thanks for playing, and we have some lovely parting gifts for you.

So why isn't there any love for the daddy in all this? Because the mommy went through the pain of carrying the load (literally) for nine plus months, and then endured the agony of birth, and now there's a days-old baby sleeping or eating or pooping and that's just so much cooler than talking to the dad.

Is anyone going to listen if you complain about being ignored? No. Should you complain anyway? No, because you were probably the center of attention when you were born, and your father was the one that was ignored. Go ahead, ask him. See if your dad was ignored after you were born because he just wasn't as interesting as a newborn baby. And if he tells you that he wasn't ignored, he's lying.

So what does all this mean? Your life has changed, my friend, and it's definitely for the better. A few rules to follow, and you should stay in good graces with your loved ones:

Rule #1: Take care of your wife first, and your child a close second. You see, if you completely devote all of your energy to your child and forget to take care of your wife some resentment may build up, and now you've got a wife who feels like she's competing with your child, and that's not right.

Take some time to spend with just your spouse, whether it's during the baby's nap time, or maybe even have a relative or friend watch the baby for an hour a week or something. But definitely make time for her, because otherwise you'll find your significant other slipping away from you, and one of the biggest reasons your baby is in this world is because of the love you and your wife share.

Got a little serious, there, huh? I don't know what got into me ... maybe my wife's been playing audio of TLC shows for me in my sleep. Onward ...

Rule #2: Take care of your child as much as your spouse does. Yes, that means changing diapers and early a.m. feedings. And by early a.m., I'm talking about the hours you used to stumble in from drinking, not the hour you get up to go to work. These are times for you to bond a little with the baby, and give your wife a chance to catch her breath. Unless you're the one staying home, feeding & changing the baby, and rocking the baby back to sleep every time it cries, she needs a break. Changing a crappy diaper or two isn't going to kill you, and feeding the baby will actually bring the two of you closer together (from a bottle, stupid, you can't lactate. And if you can, don't admit it to anyone).

Rule #3: This one's really important, but a lot of people overlook it. Sleep when the baby sleeps. During those first few weeks you're going to be up about 20 hours a day. Not too many people can function really well on that little sleep, and the only way to catch more dream time is take a nap when the baby does. This is easiest on the weekends, most difficult during the week, but you'll catch on. Pretty soon you'll be a lot like you were in college, taking mid-afternoon 45 minute snoozes two or three times a day. That'll help with the exhaustion. Trust me.

Rule #4: Learn how to just say no. Not to drugs (okay, to drugs, too), but to relatives and friends. This is especially true when you first get home from the hospital. Everyone, and I mean everyone, is going to want to stop by to meet and greet the little one. But you know what? There's only so much a days old baby can do, so you end up entertaining the visitor(s). Can I get you a drink? Something to eat? How about an early exit from our house?

You see, newborns don't do much other than eat, sleep and poop. And if the baby isn't eating or pooping your visitors really don't have much to watch, so they'll turn to you for conversation, and soon enough you'll wish you had the house to yourself again. Saying no will not only keep you from having the same conversation sixty-three times, it will also provide you with some good alone time with your spouse and your new addition. And your friends and family will understand if you don't want to have visitors rolling through all the time.

To sum up, this is one of the coolest, scariest, craziest, most confusing & happiest times in your life. Enjoy every minute of it, even the bad ones, because once that baby arrives your life will turn upside down (all for the better), and you won't be able to reclaim the time that you and significant other have just spent together.

Yes, your wife will probably gain more weight than she wants to, and she may even start resembling some circus attraction because of the way she eats, but it's a temporary condition. And her mood swings will have you on your toes for nine solid months, and her cravings will be strange, and you'll probably get relegated to the couch because her pillows will become her new snuggle buddy, but it's all worth it, right? Right.

I promise: it's all worth it.

Made in the USA